DAVID MAMET

THE OLD NEIGHBORHOOD

David Mamet was born in Chicago in 1947. He stud-
ied at Goddard College in Vermont and at the Neigh-
borhood Playhouse School of Theater in New York.
He has taught at Goddard College, the Yale School of
Drama, and New York University, and lectures at the
Atlantic Theater Company, of which he is a founding
member. He is the author of the acclaimed plays *The
Cryptogram, Oleanna, Speed-the-Plow, Glengarry Glen
Ross, American Buffalo*, and *Sexual Perversity in Chicago*.
He has also written screenplays for such films as *Homi-
cide, House of Games*, and the Oscar-nominated *The Ver-
dict*. His plays have won the Pulitzer Prize and the
Obie Award.

SCREENPLAYS

Oleanna
Glengarry Glen Ross
We're No Angels
Things Change (with Shel Silverstein)
Hoffa
The Untouchables
The Postman Always Rings Twice
The Verdict
House of Games
Homicide
Wag the Dog
The Edge
The Spanish Prisoner

THE OLD NEIGHBORHOOD

THREE PLAYS

DAVID MAMET

*The Disappearance
of the Jews*

Jolly

Deeny

VINTAGE BOOKS
A DIVISION OF RANDOM HOUSE, INC.
NEW YORK

A VINTAGE ORIGINAL

Two of the plays in this collection were previously published:
The Disappearance of the Jews was first published by Samuel
French, Inc. Copyright © 1982, 1987 by David Mamet
Jolly was first published by Applause Theatre Books in *Best
Short Plays*. Copyright © 1989 by David Mamet

Library of Congress Cataloging-in-Publication Data
Mamet, David.
The old neighborhood : three plays / by David Mamet.
p.   cm.
"A Vintage original"—T.p. verso.
Contents: The disappearance of the Jews—Jolly—Deeny.
ISBN 978-0-679-74652-2
I. Title.
PS3563.A4345O37   1998
812'.54—dc21   97-32224
CIP

www.randomhouse.com

Book design by Debbie Glasserman
Frontispiece art by Elizabeth Dahlie

Manufactured in the United States of America

146684614

CONTENTS

The Old Neighborhood was first produced on April 11, 1997, at the Hasty Pudding Theatre, in Cambridge, Massachusetts, by the American Repertory Theatre, as part of their New Stages Series, with the following cast:

Bobby:	Tony Shalhoub
Jolly:	Brooke Adams
Joey:	Vincent Guastaferro
Deeny:	Rebecca Pidgeon
Carl:	Jack Willis

Directed by Scott Zigler; sets by Kevin Rigdon; costumes by Harriet Voyt; lighting by John Ambrosone

The Old Neighborhood was produced on November 19, 1997, at the Booth Theatre, in New York, by Carole Shorenstein Hays and Stuart Thompson, with the following cast:

Bobby:	Peter Riegert
Jolly:	Patti LuPone
Joey:	Vincent Guastaferro
Deeny:	Rebecca Pidgeon
Carl:	Jack Willis

Directed by Scott Zigler; sets by Kevin Rigdon; costumes by Harriet Voyt; lighting by John Ambrosone

THE DISAPPEARANCE

OF THE JEWS

CHARACTERS

BOBBY	a man in his thirties or forties
JOEY	his friend

SCENE

A hotel room

JOEY: What I remember . . . what I remember was that time we were at Ka-Ga-Wak we took Howie Greenberg outside.

BOBBY: Was that Howie Greenberg?

JOEY: Yeah . . .

BOBBY: No . . .

JOEY: No? Who was it, then?

BOBBY: It . . .

JOEY: It was Howie Greenberg.

BOBBY: Red hair . . .

JOEY: Yeah. Red hair. Braces.

BOBBY: That was Howie Greenberg?

JOEY: Yeah.

BOBBY: From Temple Zion?

JOEY: No. He never went to Zion?

BOBBY: No?

JOEY: No. Hey, Bob, no, you never went to Zion.

BOBBY: What's that mean, I don't know who went there . . . ?

JOEY: No. It doesn't mean that. But you know the time I'm talking of?

BOBBY: We tied him to the bed. We put him in the snow.

JOEY: Yeah.

BOBBY: I got to tell you something, Joey, it was not Howie Greenberg. Howie never went to Winter Camp. *(Pause)* Am I right? *(Pause)* Am I right? Jeff went to Winter Camp. Tell me I'm wrong. *(Pause)* You fuckin' asshole . . .

JOEY: You, you, what the fuck would you know, never even get a Christmas card from you: "What happened to who." It was Jeff . . . ?

BOBBY: Yeah. *(Pause)*

JOEY: Isn't that funny . . . I'm not sure you're right . . . *(Pause)* Huh . . .

BOBBY: Whatever happened to Howie?

JOEY: Howie.

BOBBY: Yeah.

JOEY: Are you ready for this . . . ? Howie turned out to be a fag.

BOBBY: You're kidding.

JOEY: No.

BOBBY: You're kidding.

JOEY: No.

BOBBY: He's a fag.

JOEY: That he is.

BOBBY: How about that.

JOEY: Isn't that something.

BOBBY: Yeah. *(Pause)* His parents?

JOEY: Moved to Florida. *(Pause)*

BOBBY: I always liked him.

JOEY: I did, too. *(Pause)*

BOBBY: Huh. *(Pause)*

JOEY: Yeah. *(Pause)*

BOBBY: What ever happened to Jeff?

JOEY: He's still here . . .

(Pause)

JOEY: I was thinking I was up on Devon. . . . You 'member when we used to take the Ravenswood . . . ?

BOBBY: When? See the Cubs . . . ?

JOEY: Yeah.

BOBBY: Oh yeah . . . Is that joint still there?

JOEY: What? Frankels . . . ?

BOBBY: On Devon . . . ?

JOEY: The roast beef . . . ?

BOBBY: Yeah.

JOEY: Yeah. It's still there. It isn't on Devon.

BOBBY: No?

JOEY: It's on Petersen. It's in Rogers Park. *(Pause)*

BOBBY: You 'member those two broads we had?

JOEY: The Rogers Park broads?

BOBBY: The folk dancing broads . . .

JOEY: . . . yeah . . .

BOBBY: The two Debbies . . .

JOEY: Debbie. Yeah. Right.

BOBBY: Rubovitz and Rosen.

JOEY: Debbie Rubovitz and Rosen.

BOBBY: For five bucks, which one was mine?

JOEY: I don't know.

BOBBY: For ten bucks?

JOEY: Rosen.

BOBBY: You're full of shit.

JOEY: Rosen. You owe me ten bucks.

BOBBY: It wasn't Rosen.

JOEY: You don't know, you fuck, you're bullshitting me. You don't remember.

BOBBY: I remember. Mine was Rosen.

JOEY: That's what I said.

BOBBY: No.

JOEY: You said, "Which one was Rosen." I said yours.

BOBBY: She was? *(Pause)*

JOEY: I don't remember . . .

BOBBY: Which was the short one . . . ?

JOEY: Yours. Right? With the curly hair . . . ?

BOBBY: And which one was her name?

JOEY: I don't know. *(Pause)*

BOBBY: Whatever you think happened to those broads?

JOEY: I don't know.

BOBBY: You ever think about them?

JOEY: Very seldom. When I go through Rogers Park. *(Pause)*

BOBBY: You think they were dykes?

JOEY: I don't know. D'you think that?

BOBBY: I kind of did.

JOEY: I kind of did, too.

BOBBY: At the time?

JOEY: No. Are you kidding me . . . ? Who knew? I tell you what I think: They were before their time.

BOBBY: Oh yeah . . . they were . . .

JOEY: They were before their time. . . .

BOBBY: Fucking broads.

JOEY: I tell you how I always knew the broad was yours, the broad she couldn't find her way outta the bathroom, that was yours . . .

BOBBY: And what were you, a head man . . . ?

JOEY: Except for Deeny, of course.

BOBBY: . . . what . . . ?

JOEY: Except for Deeny. Yes, I was a head man, yeah . . .

BOBBY: You wanted to discuss, what . . . ?

JOEY: . . . and the broad, she couldn't find the light switch, that was yours . . .

BOBBY: . . . okay . . .

JOEY: "Why's this black stuff coming out of the salt shaker?"

BOBBY: . . . some intellectual giants . . .

JOEY: . . . that's right . . .

BOBBY: "Tell us about Moby Dick" . . .

JOEY: You wished . . .

BOBBY: And so which broad was mine?

JOEY: Rosen . . . I don't know . . . Rubovitz . . . Some Jew broad . . . some folk dancer. I don't know . . . some JAP . . . some Eskimo . . .   (*Pause*) How's Laurie?

BOBBY: Fine.

JOEY: Yeah, but how is she, though . . . ?

BOBBY: She's fine. What did I say?

JOEY: You said that she was fine. (*Pause*)

BOBBY: All right. (*Pause*)

JOEY: So? (*Pause*)

BOBBY: So what?

JOEY: Yeah. So what, so how is she, you give me this shit all the time . . . you never fuckin' changed you know that, Bob: "Fuck you, I don't need anyone, fuck you" . . .

BOBBY: And what are you, huh? You been reading *Redbook* . . . ? What is this all of a sudden . . . (*Pause*) You want to know how she is? She's fine.

JOEY: Well, that's all I asked. I ast you how she is, you barked at me. Fuck you.

BOBBY: Hey, you know, Joey, you know, people get married . . .

JOEY: Yeah. I know they do.

BOBBY: They . . . *(Pause)*

JOEY: What? *(Pause)* What? *(Pause)* What? Mr. Wisdom . . . speak to me.

BOBBY: I should never have married a shiksa.

JOEY: Yeah. I know. 'Cause that's all that you used to say, "Let's find some Jew broads and discuss the Talmud . . ."

BOBBY: This is something different.

JOEY: Is it?

BOBBY: Yes. I'm talking about marriage, you asked a question, I'm answering you. You don't want to fuckin' talk about it, we'll talk about something that you like. *(Pause)*

JOEY: Tell me.

12

BOBBY: You know what she said?

JOEY: Who, Laurie?

BOBBY: Yeah.

JOEY: No, what.

BOBBY: Listen to this: "What are we going to tell the kids."

JOEY: She said that?

BOBBY: Yes.

JOEY: When?

BOBBY: Right before I left . . .

JOEY: "What are you going to tell the kids . . . ?"

BOBBY: Yeah. *(Pause)*

JOEY: What *are* you going to tell the kids?

BOBBY: What is there to tell? The kid is a Jew.

JOEY: *(Pause)* Well, Bob, the law says he's a Jew, his, you know what the law says, he's a Jew his mother is a Jew.

BOBBY: Fuck the law.

JOEY: Well, all I'm saying, that's what the law says . . .

BOBBY: Joey, Joey, what are you saying, a kid of mine isn't going to be a Jew? What is he going to be? Look at him . . .

JOEY: I'm, I'm only talking about . . .

BOBBY: I know what you're talking about. What I'm saying, common sense? They start knocking heads in the schoolyard looking for Jews, you fuckin' think they aren't going to take my kid because of, uh . . .

JOEY: No. No.

BOBBY: Well . . . ?

JOEY: What I'm saying . . .

BOBBY: . . . are they going to take him, or they're going to pass him up 'cause he's so . . .

JOEY: I'm talking about the law.

BOBBY: 'Cause he's so blond and all, "Let's go beat up some kikes. . . . Oh, not *that* kid. . . ."

JOEY: Hey, Bobby, don't make me out the bad guy here, I only brought it up.

BOBBY: Well, listen to this, Joe, because I want to tell you what she says to me one night: "If you've been persecuted so long, eh, you must have brought it on yourself." *(Pause)*

JOEY: She said that?

BOBBY: Yes. *(Pause)*

JOEY: Wait a second. If we've been oppressed so long we must be doing it.

BOBBY: *(Pause)* Yes.

JOEY: She said that.

BOBBY: Yes. *(Pause)*

JOEY: And what did you say to her?

BOBBY: I don't know . . .

JOEY: What do you mean you don't know? What did you say to her?

BOBBY: Nothing. *(Pause)*

JOEY: She actually said that? *(Pause)*

BOBBY: And *(Pause)* And I mean it got me thinking . . .

JOEY: Ho, ho, ho, ho, hold on a minute, here, ho, Bobby. Lemme tell you something. Let me tell you what she feels: She feels left out, Jim. Don't let that white shit get into your head. She feels left out. They got, what have they got, you talk about community, six droll cocksuckers at a lawn party somewhere: "How is your boat . . . ?" Fuck that shit, fuck that shit, she's got a point in my ass, what the fuck did they ever do? They can't make a joke for chrissake. I'll tell you something, you're sitting down, the reason that the goyim hate us the whole time, in addition they were envious is; we don't descend to their level . . . *(Pause)* because we wouldn't fight. The reason we were persecuted because we said, hey, all right, leave me alone, those Nordic types, all right, these football players, these cocksuckers in a fuckin', wrapped in hides come down and 'cause we don't fight back they go "Who are those people . . . ?" *(Pause)* "Hey, let's hit them in the head." Because we have our mind on higher things. *(Pause)* Because we got something better to do than all day to fuckin' beat the women up and go kill things. My dad would puke to hear you talk that way. I swear to God. Alavasholem, he would weep with blood, your father, too, to hear you go that way. What are they doing to you out there? *(Pause)* You're too shut off, Bob. You should come back here. *(Pause)* My dad. *(Pause)* You

16

know, when we were growing up, he always used to say: It will happen again. We used to say, huh . . . ?

BOBBY: I remember.

JOEY: I used to say, "Papa, you're here now. It's over." He would say, "It will happen in your lifetime." And I used to think he was a fool. But I know he was right. *(Pause)* I'm sorry that now he isn't here to tell him so. *(Pause)* Because I wish he was here. *(Pause)*

BOBBY: 'V'you been out to Waldheim?

JOEY: Judy and I went last month. We try to go once a month.

BOBBY: Would you like to go out?

JOEY: We could go. Yes.

BOBBY: Just the two of us.

JOEY: I know what you're saying.

BOBBY: When can we go?

JOEY: How long will you be in town?

BOBBY: Till the weekend.

JOEY: You want to go tomorrow?

BOBBY: Yes.

JOEY: All right. *(Pause)* We'll go in the morning. *(Pause)*

BOBBY: I'll pick you up.

JOEY: All right.

BOBBY: We're really going to go.

JOEY: All right.

(Pause)

JOEY: I'll tell you something else: I would have been a great man in Europe—I was meant to be hauling stones, or setting fence posts, something. . . . Look at me: the way I'm built, and here I'm working in a fucking restaurant my whole life. No wonder I'm fat. I swear to God. You know how strong I am? We went to Judy's folks, they had a tree had fallen in the road. Up in Wisconsin . . . ?

BOBBY: Yeah . . . ?

JOEY: I picked it up. *(Pause)* They wanted me to take a crowbar to shove it aside, the car could pass. I didn't

18

know what they meant. Huh? I wasn't showing off . . .
you know I'm strong . . .

BOBBY: . . . since grade school.

JOEY: And Arthur says, "We got to move the tree . . ." I
picked it up, I put it over there, I put it down, he's
standing there, a crowbar, all their mouths are hung
open. (Pause) It was a big tree, too. That's what I
mean, Bobby, that's where we should be, farming
somewhere. . . . Building things, carrying things . . .
this shit is dilute, this is schveck this shit, I swear to
God, the doctors, teachers, everybody, in the law, the
writers all the time geschraiying, all those assholes,
how they're lost . . . of course, they're lost. They
should be studying talmud . . . we should be able to
come to them and to say, "What is the truth . . . ?"
And they should tell us. What the talmud says, what
this one said, what Hillel said, and I, I should be
working on a forge all day. They'd say, "There goes
Reb Lewis, he's the strongest man in Lodz." I'd nod.
"He once picked up an ox." (Pause) Or some fucking
thing. I don't know if you can pick up an ox, Bob, but
I tell you, I feel in my heart I was meant to work out
in the winter all day. To be strong. Of course we're
schlepping all the time with heart attacks, with fat,
look at this goddam food I sell . . . that stuff will kill
you, it killed my dad . . . it's good to harvest wheat, to
forge, to toil; my father's sitting on his ass for forty
years driving through Idaho for Green and Green,

what did he need for nourishment . . . ? Nothin'. He should have been . . . the time should come we're sixty we look back, our wives are there, our children, the community . . . and we are sitting there, we are something. . . . And we've been men. You know . . . ?

BOBBY: Yes.

JOEY: And we've lived. We've lived the life we were supposed to live. *(Pause)* Not this, Bobby. Not this . . . *(Pause)* I don't know. I'm getting old. I look at the snow the only thing I long that I should be in Europe.

BOBBY: I'm sure it was no picnic there.

JOEY: In Europe?

BOBBY: Yes.

JOEY: Ah, fuck, I don't know, Bob . . . I don't know . . .

BOBBY: Joe, with the Nazis . . . ?

JOEY: Fuck the Nazis. Fuck the Nazis, Bob. I'm saying, give a guy a chance to stand up. . . . Give 'im something to stand for.

BOBBY: That's very pretty, and when they stick glass rods in your dick and break them off . . .

JOEY: . . . that was the Japs . . .

BOBBY: I'm saying, Joey, that's romantic shit . . .

JOEY: Is it . . . ?

BOBBY: Because, yes, because, yes. It is. And to a certain, yes, it is, and to a certain extent it's, I'll tell you what it's, it's profaning what they went through.

JOEY: Oh. Is it . . . ?

BOBBY: Yes.

JOEY: And why . . .

BOBBY: Because they went through it.

JOEY: They did . . . what I'm saying, that I could have, too, that's all I'm saying.

BOBBY: You don't know you could have . . .

JOEY: Yes. That's what I'm saying, Bob . . . I could . . .

BOBBY: . . . to go through that shit in the Camps . . . ?

JOEY: Yes.

BOBBY: No, Joe, no. You don't know what you would have done. . . . *(JOEY shrugs.)* You don't know what the fuck you would have done, what you would have felt. None of us know.

JOEY: *(Shrugs)* If you say so, Bob.

(Pause)

JOEY: I'll tell you where I would of loved it: in the shtetl. *(Pause)* I would of loved it there. You, too. You would of been Reb Gould. You would of told them what Rabbi Akiba said . . .

BOBBY: You think they fooled around?

JOEY: Who? In the shtetl?

BOBBY: Yeah.

JOEY: The guys in the shtetl?

BOBBY: Yeah.

JOEY: I think it was too small.

BOBBY: But when they went to town . . .

JOEY: When the guys went to town?

BOBBY: Yes.

JOEY: With Polish whores . . . ?

BOBBY: Yeah . . .

JOEY: I don't know.

BOBBY: You think you would have?

JOEY: No. With who?

BOBBY: Or some young Jewish thing . . . ?

JOEY: Inside the shtetl . . . ?

BOBBY: Yes.

JOEY: And, what, defile my home . . . ?

BOBBY: You think you would have.

JOEY: You would be found out . . .

BOBBY: I would?

JOEY: Because you were a, yeah. Because you were a Jew. If you wanted to go out fuck around who'd have you? If you stayed home you would be found out. I think,

(Pause) But on the other hand who's to say what could go on. At night. In Europe. *(Pause)* That's true, too . . . *(Pause)* Judy would be old . . . she would have some incurable disease . . . we would be married years. But I would not be old. I would be deep in grief, and deep in contemplation of my life. Some young, the daughter of one of my customers, the orphaned daughter . . . is this what you're saying?

BOBBY: Yes.

JOEY: She comes to me, the whole town is silent with sympathy, "I baked this for you." *(Pause)*

BOBBY: Righty-o. *(Pause)*

JOEY: Is this what you're saying?

BOBBY: That's right. What did she bake?

JOEY: What did she bake? What did she bake? What did she bake?

BOBBY: *(Pause)* . . . yum.

JOEY: *(Pause)* . . . carbohydrates . . .

(Pause)

JOEY: Yeah, many times I wished to go back, to the war, to when my folks came here . . . to Orchard Street . . . you know, to Maxwell Street . . . to pushcarts . . . to . . .

BOBBY: We wouldn't have liked it.

JOEY: You think?

BOBBY: No.

JOEY: I don't know . . .

BOBBY: You know what I would, I'll tell you what I would have loved, to go, in the twenties, to be in Hollywood . . .

JOEY: Huh.

BOBBY: Jesus, I know they had a good time there. Here you got, I mean, five smart Jew boys from Russia, this whole industry . . .

JOEY: Who?

BOBBY: Who. Mayer. Warners. Fox.

JOEY: Fox? Fox is Jewish?

BOBBY: Sure.

JOEY: Fox is a Jewish name?

BOBBY: Sure.

JOEY: Who knew that?

BOBBY: Everyone.

JOEY: Huh. *(Pause)* I always saw their thing, it looked goyish to me.

BOBBY: What thing?

JOEY: Their castle, that thing on their movies . . .

BOBBY: No.

JOEY: I thought it was a goyish name.

BOBBY: "Fox"?

JOEY: Twentieth Century-Fox. *(Pause)* Century Fox. *(Pause)* Charlie Chaplin was Jewish.

BOBBY: I know that, Joe.

JOEY: Yeah? People fool you. Oh, you know, you know who else was Jewish? Mr. White . . .

BOBBY: Mr. White . . . ?

JOEY: Mr. White. On Jeffrey. The shoe store . . . ?
Miller-White Shoes.

BOBBY: . . . yeah . . . ?

JOEY: On Jeffrey . . . ?

BOBBY: He was Jewish?

JOEY: Yeah.

BOBBY: Huh.

JOEY: My mom told me.

BOBBY: He didn't look Jewish.

JOEY: That's what I'm saying . . . *(Pause)*

BOBBY: He was a nice guy.

JOEY: Yes. He was.

BOBBY: I remember him. They always gave you what, a
lollipop something when you came out.

JOEY: Why do you think kids hate trying on shoes?

BOBBY: I don't know. *(Pause)* You know, actually I don't like trying them on either.

JOEY: You don't?

BOBBY: No. *(Pause)*

JOEY: I don't think that I do either. *(Pause)* Jimmy does.

BOBBY: He does?

JOEY: Yeah. *(Pause)* So I was reminiscing with my mom . . .

BOBBY: . . . yeah . . .

JOEY: You know, about the shoe store, huh? 'Cause I took Jimmy in to get his shoes, I'm talking about when we stopped on Pratt, I say, "The old shoestore the goyish guy, Miller's partner." So she goes "Jerry White . . ." He was the shamus, Temple Zion thirty years.

BOBBY: Huh.

JOEY: Huh . . . ?

BOBBY: How about that.

JOEY: That's what I said.

BOBBY: How about that. *(Pause)* He still alive?

JOEY: No. He died.

BOBBY: He died, huh?

JOEY: Yes. He did. *(Pause)*

BOBBY: The store still there?

JOEY: Oh, Bobby, it's all gone. It's all gone there. You knew that . . .

(Pause)

JOEY: Life is too short.

BOBBY: Life is very short.

JOEY: It's very short. We're sitting on the stoop, we're old . . . *(Pause)* We're married . . . we have kids . . . *(Pause)*

BOBBY: How's Judy?

JOEY: *(Pause)* I pray, you know, I pray every night, I pray that I can get through life without murdering anybody.

BOBBY: Who would you murder?

JOEY: I'm saying I'm uncontrollable.

BOBBY: Hey, hey, you're human . . .

JOEY: . . . and I got married wrong. *(Pause)* Well . . .
there, *(Pause)* there you are.

BOBBY: You didn't get married wrong, Joe.

JOEY: Yes, I did. You don't know. I want to tell you something, Bob, she's a wonderful woman, but there's such
a thing as lust. I don't know if it's lust. Yes. Yes, it is. I,
I, I say this is a feeling . . . I, I'm not alone. *(Pause)*
Then I walk out the door . . .

BOBBY: We all feel like that sometimes . . .

JOEY: You don't know what I'm going to say, I walk out of
the door I say, "If I never saw them again, it would be
fine . . ."

BOBBY: We all feel like that sometimes . . .

JOEY: No, no. Listen to me. There are times, a feeling I
think gets so overpowering it becomes a fact, and you
don't even know you did it. Sometimes I think, "Well

if they were killed . . . if they died . . ." and sometimes I think I'll do it myself.

BOBBY: It's just a feeling, Joe.

JOEY: I pray you'll never know it. Sometimes it goes farther. I have killed them, and I take the plane, I don't call anyone, because now I don't care; and fly to Canada and rent a car and go into the forest and begin to walk . . . I know I have to die . . . so I walk . . . and I'm going north. I feel so free. I can't tell you, Bobby . . . I have a pistol, I can end it any time. I feel so free . . . If I could feel like that in my life . . . I swear there are people who can live like that. I know there are. Who exist. Holy men. Visionaries, scholars, I know they exist. . . . I know they're cloistered. . . . I know that it's real. But I can't get it up. I'm going to die like this. A shmuck. *(Pause)* All of the stuff I'd like to do. I'll never do it. *(Pause)* What do you make of that? *(Long pause)*

BOBBY: You really have a gun?

JOEY: What gun?

BOBBY: You said you have a pistol . . .

JOEY: I said that I have a pistol . . . ?

BOBBY: You said you were going north . . .

31

JOEY: In my dream. In my dream . . . in my fantasy . . .
you know . . .

BOBBY: Oh. *(Pause)*

JOEY: In my imaginings.

BOBBY: Oh. *(Pause)*

JOEY: I actually *have* a pistol. In my store.

BOBBY: You do?

JOEY: Behind the counter.

BOBBY: Mmm.

JOEY: For burglars. You worried I would shoot myself?

BOBBY: You said you would.

JOEY: I actually might. I think that sometimes. *(Pause)*
Don't you? *(Pause)* Bobby . . . ?

BOBBY: *(Pause)* Sometimes. *(Pause)*

JOEY: I knew you did. *(Pause)* I wouldn't take the pistol
from the store, though. And I'll tell you why, because
I think that just its presence, that you know it's there

32

discourages them. *(Pause)* Let them go rob someplace else. Everything, everything, everything . . . it's . . . I'll tell you: It's a mystery . . . *(Pause)* Everything is a mystery, Bob . . . everything. *(Pause)* I don't know how things work. I can hang up a coat hook, people that I know can fix a stove. *(Pause)* Anyone can change a tire—although Lucille bought a new Pontiac, she went to change the tire, the jack wouldn't fit it.

BOBBY: Maybe she wasn't putting it in right.

JOEY: She said that she was. I think they gave her the wrong size, they custom things today and you can't change a fucking tire with the wrong size jack. People could die of something like that. Because everything is so far from us today. And we have no connection.

BOBBY: There are people who have a connection.

JOEY: Who? Who are they? . . . and there are lives, Bobby, where people never have a thought. Where all day it is like they aren't there. Where they are a dream of their environment. Where their lives are a joy. Where questions are answered with ritual. Where life is short. We read them in the books.

BOBBY: . . . what books . . . ?

JOEY: I don't know what books . . . that's what I'm saying . . . but there are things . . . there are things . . .

there ... there are ways to get there that exist. They ... *(Pause)* In rituals, I'm saying that you didn't make up, but existed ... they would cause you pain.

BOBBY: Who would?

JOEY: ... they'd take you in a hut. You'd come out, you would be a man. *(Pause)* And, by God, that is what you would be. *(Pause)*

BOBBY: *(Pause)* I think I invent ceremonies, but I never keep them up. I know I should, I say if I forget this now, I'll never keep it up, but I don't.

JOEY: What? Like what?

BOBBY: Like anything.

JOEY: Like what?

BOBBY: Like prayer.

JOEY: You don't keep up prayer?

BOBBY: No.

JOEY: What? Did you used to pray?

BOBBY: I've prayed. *(Pause)*

JOEY: Judy and I joined a synagogue.

BOBBY: You did?

JOEY: Yeah.

BOBBY: Which one?

JOEY: It's new.

BOBBY: Up by you?

JOEY: Yeah. *(Pause)*

BOBBY: What do you do, you go there . . .

JOEY: . . . we just joined . . .

BOBBY: You did.

JOEY: Yeah. *(Pause)*

BOBBY: Hey, you know?

JOEY: Yeah, I know.

BOBBY: What?

JOEY: I know.

BOBBY: *(Sigh)* Joey . . . Joey . . . Joey.

JOEY: Bushes are steel.

BOBBY: Bushes are steel. What else in the world would they be?

JOEY: That's right.

BOBBY: And what's the second manhole?

JOEY: It's a ground rule double.

BOBBY: Take your base. *(Pause)* D'you ever think that we would live to be this old?

JOEY: No. *(Pause)* I never thought about it. *(Pause)*

BOBBY: You think we're getting old?

JOEY: Yeah. *(Pause)* I suppose we are. *(Pause)* Isn't everybody?

(Pause)

BOBBY: You remember the Sleepy Time Motel?

JOEY: Yes.

BOBBY: Is it still there?

JOEY: Yes, it is.

BOBBY: You remember when Joan Carpenter threw up?

JOEY: Yes.

BOBBY: Those girls. *(Pause)*

JOEY: Yeah, I remember . . .

BOBBY: *(Pause)* Joan . . . Deeny.

JOEY: Deeny. I see her now and then. She works at Fields.

BOBBY: She does?

JOEY: She got divorced.

BOBBY: I didn't even know that she was married.

JOEY: She got married million years ago.

BOBBY: When did she get divorced?

JOEY: Not too long, maybe a year ago. Two years.

BOBBY: And how is she?

JOEY: Yeah. She's fine.

BOBBY: Did she get fat?

JOEY: No. *(Pause)* She's selling cosmetics on the first floor.

BOBBY: She is?

JOEY: Yeah.

BOBBY: She ever ask about me?

JOEY: Yeah.

BOBBY: What does she say?

JOEY: How were you.

BOBBY: What did you tell her?

JOEY: That you're fine. *(Pause)*

BOBBY: She works at the place downtown or on Michigan?

JOEY: Michigan.

BOBBY: Cosmetics.

JOEY: Yeah.

BOBBY: What does she look like?

JOEY: She looks the same.

BOBBY: She does?

JOEY: Yeah. I'm struck by that sometimes. I mean you look the same to me.

BOBBY: Isn't that funny, 'cause you look the same to me.

JOEY: You think that's funny?

BOBBY: Yeah.

JOEY: I think it's funny, too. I wish I had a cigarette.

BOBBY: Yes. I do, too. *(Beat)*

JOEY: You wanna go get some?

BOBBY: I almost do, but I shouldn't.

JOEY: No, I shouldn't either. *(Pause)* Isn't that something?

BOBBY: Yes. It is, Joe.

JOEY: Isn't that something?

BOBBY: It's one for the books.

END

JOLLY

CHARACTERS

JOLLY	a woman in her thirties or forties
BOB	her brother
CARL	her husband

SCENE

Jolly's home

SCENE ONE

Evening. JOLLY, BOB, *and* CARL.

JOLLY: . . . and he said, "I disapprove of you." "Of what?"
I said. "Of, well, I don't know if I want to go into
it . . ." "Of something I've done . . . ?" I said, "Yes."
"To you?" "No." "To *whom?*" I said. He said he would
much rather not take it up. "Well, I wish you *would*
take it up," I said, "because it's important to me." "It's
the way," he said. "It's the way that you are with your
children."

BOB: *(Pause) What? (Pause)*

JOLLY: "It's the way that you are with your children."

BOB: Oh, Lord . . .

JOLLY: I . . .

BOB: . . . how long can this go . . .

JOLLY: I . . .

BOB: . . . how long can this go *on?*

43

JOLLY: I wanted to, you know, I stayed on the pho—

BOB: How long can this go on? *Wait a* minute. *Wait* a minute: You should call all . . .

JOLLY: . . . I know . . .

BOB: . . . you should cease . . .

JOLLY: . . . I know.

BOB: . . . all *meetings, dialogue* . . .

JOLLY: . . . but the children . . .

BOB: You should never . . . listen to me, Jolly:

JOLLY: I'm . . .

BOB: You sh—

JOLLY: Yes, I know.

BOB: You should take an oath never to *talk* to, *meet* with . . .

JOLLY: . . . but the children . . .

BOB: And the children most especially. How can this, are

we going to expose another generation to this . . . this . . .

JOLLY: And the thing of it is, is . . .

BOB: He said *what? What* did he say . . . ?

JOLLY: He . . .

BOB: He didn't like the way you raise your children . . .

JOLLY: . . . he said that he'd been in *therapy* . . .

BOB: . . . hu.

JOLLY: . . . and he'd, he'd come to . . . *what* was it . . . ?

CARL: "See."

JOLLY: . . . he was a different *man.* From the man we knew.

CARL: He'd come to "realize" that he had "changed."

JOLLY: . . . to realize that he had changed, yes, and the things which, in a prior life, he might have "suppressed" . . .

BOB: . . . that's their way. That's their way. That's their

swinish, selfish, *goddam* them. What *treachery* have
they not done, in the name of . . .

JOLLY: . . . I know . . .

BOB: . . . of "honesty." God *damn* them. And always
"telling" us we . . .

JOLLY: . . . yes.

BOB: . . . we were the bad ones . . .

JOLLY: Well, we were.

BOB: . . . *we* were the bad ones.

JOLLY: And when he said it, I heard his father's voice.

BOB: Well, *fuck* him . . .

JOLLY: And I saw. He'd turned into his father.

BOB: . . . he didn't like the way you raise your kids . . .

JOLLY: And so, you know, I knew, I *remembered*. Way
back. They were . . .

BOB: . . . they were sweet kids.

JOLLY: *He* was a sweet kid.

BOB: . . . she . . . ?

JOLLY: *He* was a sweet kid, Buub. You weren't there . . .

BOB: I was there for part of it.

JOLLY: NO. You weren't there, you know. You weren't there. *I* was there. I see where it all comes from. Both of them, the traits . . .

BOB: . . . Yes.

JOLLY: . . . and they had . . . I don't mean to excuse them. I don't want to *excuse* them.

BOB: . . . there's no excuse for them.

JOLLY: No. I believe that. And I am not a vindictive person.

BOB: No.

JOLLY: I'm not, Buub. I've been thinking of this . . .

BOB: I know that you're not.

JOLLY: And I think about all those years . . .

BOB: They treated you like filth. *(Pause)*

JOLLY: Yes. They did. They treated me like filth. Do you know, you don't know, 'cause you weren't there—when they first came. *Mother* told me, I was ten. So she was, what eight; she was going to sleep in my bed. She took up the bed, as she was a "creeper," you know. I'm a rock. You put me in a bed. And unmoving. Morning. She was all over the place. And I went in and told Mom that I couldn't sleep. She said, "She is his daughter, and this is the case. If you can't sleep, sleep on the floor."

BOB: No.

JOLLY: . . . and . . . yes. And she wouldn't let me take the covers. *(Pause)*

CARL: . . . and she wanted to call him back.

BOB: Call him back.

CARL: Yes.

BOB: And say *what?*

JOLLY: I was so . . . *astonished.* By the phone call . . .

BOB: Someone calls me up, says, "I don't like the way you raise your kids . . ."

JOLLY: I was, you know, like sometimes when you are in *shock* . . . ?

BOB: . . . yes.

JOLLY: The most bizarre events seem "commonplace."

BOB: . . . yes.

JOLLY: I was . . . because you know, I called HIM. He didn't call *me*, I called him. *This was the thing of it:* The kids. My kids. They were *close* to him. When he and Susan first got married . . .

BOB: . . . yes . . .

JOLLY: They used to, they'd say: "What do your kids like to do? What are a list of their favorite . . ."

CARL: . . . activities.

JOLLY: . . . and we would write them *down* . . . and they would come over and take the kids, and take the *list* and do all of them.

BOB: Hm.

JOLLY: Do *all* of them. Five things in a day and they'd do *all* of 'em . . . and *loved* the kids. So. Since we've moved. And we had not *heard* from them. For six months. So I picked up the phone . . .

BOB: . . . that was your mistake.

JOLLY: I picked up the phone. And I called them. "How are you? Sorry we haven't . . . 'called' you". . . and the stress of *moving* . . ."pause." Is there something *wrong?* Is something the *matter?* No. He doesn't want to talk about it. "What is it?" and then . . .

BOB: And then you have to wrench it from him . . . Please *tell* me . . ."

JOLLY: The "counseling." He's "*changed.*" . . . He's come to see.

BOB: . . . uh huh . . .

JOLLY: How he was re—

BOB: He was repressing his feelings.

JOLLY: Yes. He was repressing his—

BOB: About the way you raise your kids . . . ?

JOLLY: Well, you know, and the *counseling*, and *she* is in the counseling and all this psychobabble. And they never took "responsibility" for any aspect of the things, you know, the things that they were "feeling." . . . It's all . . . "I." "Me." "What I feel." Oh, oh, he said he's learning—you're going to love this: He's learning to live "facing his past."

BOB: Facing his past.

JOLLY: Facing his past.

BOB: Well, of course. Of course. That's how they *all* live. Facing the past. Facing the past. Looking at the past. *Fuck* him. AND fuck "counseling," is the thing I'm saying . . .

JOLLY: . . . I'm with you.

BOB: Fucking leeches.

JOLLY: "Counseling."

BOB: Hey? Y'don't need a *roofing* counselor. You need, you may need a *roofer*, tell you "get a new roof." You don't need, *sit* there, five years, five hours a week, *talking* about "Do we need a roof. Do we need a roof." *(Pause)*

CARL: Tell him. *(Pause)*

JOLLY: You know, he told me, when he did Mom's estate . . . ?

BOB: Her estate? She never had a thing of her own, her whole life.

JOLLY: Hold on. I went to him, you know, all her antiques . . . ?

BOB: He's selling them. I know.

JOLLY: He *sold* them.

BOB: . . . he sold them?

JOLLY: He *sold* them. He kept saying, "Anything you want, just *tell* me . . ."

BOB: . . . he sold them . . . ?

CARL: Yes.

JOLLY: So I *told* him. Everything I said . . .

BOB: . . . oh, no.

JOLLY: You know, and anything I'd ask for . . .

BOB: . . . yes.

JOLLY: He'd say, "Waaaaalll . . . , that's a very special *piece* . . . uh. Huh huh." What do I get? NOTHING. NOTHING. Nothing. Some cheap . . . and it doesn't *matter. (Pause)* But she was my mother. And I was there while she was dying. *I* was there. *I* was there. He'd drop her off, and I was left, an infirm woman. Fourteen hours a day. And when she'd wake up at night, and my two kids, and no "Nurse," no. And he could afford it . . . *I* couldn't . . .

BOB: . . . no . . .

JOLLY: *He* could. And just drop her off. And sonofabitch that *cunt* that *cunt* that *Carol.* DIDN'T EVEN COME TO THE . . .

BOB: . . . I know . . .

JOLLY: . . . the *funeral.* And who gets the armoire?

BOB: Which?

JOLLY: In the hallway. And who gets the mink coat? *(Pause)*

BOB: . . . I know . . .

JOLLY: Couldn't spare the time . . .

BOB: . . . yes . . .

JOLLY: . . . from her *counselors* . . . who are, what, going to teach her how to Lead a Good Life . . . ? Fuck HER. And all the married *men* she's screwing. As her way. Of expressing herself, and could not even come to Mom's *funeral.* And he says, "What do you want, Jolly . . . ? And I *tell* him.

BOB: . . . yes . . .

JOLLY: Nothing very valuable, God forbid, except that it had a meaning for me. AND EVERY PIECE, Buuby, that I say . . .

BOB: . . . I know . . .

JOLLY: He tells me *why I cannot have it.* Until . . .

BOB: . . . of course . . .

JOLLY: I stop asking.

BOB: . . . I know . . .

JOLLY: . . . because . . .

BOB: . . . I know, Jol . . .

JOLLY: . . . because, because . . . *(Pause)* So . . . so . . . he sold them. *(Pause)*

CARL: Tell him about the money.

JOLLY: I don't care about the money.

CARL: Tell him.

JOLLY: *(Sighs)* So he says. So he says . . .

CARL: He's "sold" the stuff . . .

JOLLY: So he says the proceeds are in an "estate."

CARL: A trust.

BOB: A trust, I know.

JOLLY: So he says . . . *I* say, you know, we are having some tight times, we could really *use* some of the money . . .

BOB: . . . uh huh . . .

JOLLY: "It's in a trust." Uh huh. Round and round. Then he says, "I could, you know, perhaps I could *invade* the trust . . ."

BOB: . . . invade the trust . . .

JOLLY: Yes. "If it's . . . if it's truly . . ."

BOB: . . . why did it have to be "truly" . . . ?

JOLLY: Wait. It gets worse. *(Sighs)* So. Round and round. I call. You know. This and that. The *kids*. "I really could *use* the money. We are really—you know . . . '*moving*' . . ."

BOB: . . . yes.

JOLLY: . . . when we thought we were moving . . .

BOB: I know.

JOLLY: "And we're really *tight* now . . ." *(Pause)* "And we could use some help."

BOB: . . . I know what it cost. To ask him.

JOLLY: For "ten thousand dollars" . . . *(Pause)* the way he lives. "Ten thousand dollars" . . . Long long pause. "Waal . . ." I jump in. Whatever it took, that it took, out of the "will," I don't mean the will, what do I mean, the . . . ?

CARL: . . . estate.

JOLLY: The "estate." "Whatever it took, out of the estate. From . . ."

BOB: . . . God damn him.

JOLLY: . . . from Bill and Carol . . .

BOB: *(Softly)* God damn him . . .

JOLLY: "Whatever it took, just, if I have to *sign* something, I'll sign whatever . . ."

BOB: . . . yes.

JOLLY: ". . . and subtract . . ."

BOB: . . . of course . . .

JOLLY: "And just give me my 'portion' *now*. *(Pause)* And we really *need* it." *(Pause)* Because we did.

BOB: . . . I know you did.

JOLLY: And he says "no." *(Pause)* Just "no." *(Pause)* Just "no."

CARL: She asked him to invade the trust and he said, "No." *(Pause)*

JOLLY: . . . Oh. Oh. And it gets better. He didn't say, "No." He said . . . he said, "I am not convinced I would invade the trust if I *could*." *(Pause)*

BOB: What does that mean?

JOLLY: Well, *that's* what it means. *(Pause)* Are you hungry, Carl?

CARL: A little.

JOLLY: Mmm. I'll get it in a minute.

CARL: All right. *(Pause.* JOLLY *sighs.)*

BOB: How are you doing, Carl?

CARL: I'm fine.

BOB: Holding on?

CARL: Oh, yeah. I'm holding on. *(Pause)* How about you Bob? *(Pause)*

BOB: You ever get tired of this? You must. It's the same. Isn't it? Every year.

CARL: . . . it's the same . . .

BOB: . . . our family.

CARL: Yes. It's the same.

BOB: Don't you get tired of it?

CARL: Well, I tell you . . . *(Pause)*

BOB: Yes . . . ?

CARL: It's what it is, Bob.

JOLLY: And they made fun of us.

BOB: They . . .

JOLLY: You know they did. Carl and me. "*Jolly* . . ."

BOB: Uh huh . . .

JOLLY: "I'm sure that he's a fine 'man,' Carl . . ."

BOB: Uh huh . . .

JOLLY: "But 'we want to say' . . ."

BOB: *(To self)* "We want to say . . ."

JOLLY: "Your mother and I want to say . . ."

BOB: Well, that was how they were . . .

JOLLY: *Wasn't* it . . .

BOB: Yes.

JOLLY: *Wasn't* it?

BOB: Yes.

JOLLY: And . . . the shit at Christmas. You know, you know, Marshall Fields . . . ? She would take me to Fields. "What do you think?" Some dress. If I *wanted* the dress, I would have to say "naaaaah." She would take me back. "I think it rather suits you." "No, uh . . . it's . . . it's 'pretty,' Mom, *but* . . ." And of course, she would *buy* it for me. But if I said, "God, what a gorgeous dress." Hey. You know what? Hey, you know what I'm going to *tell* you something: "fuck her, *though* she's dead." *(Pause)* Fuck *her*, and fuck the *lot* of 'em.

BOB: . . . they never loved us.

JOLLY: They, no, Buub, in their "way" . . .

BOB: Jol, Jol, that's, that's your *problem* . . .

JOLLY: What is? What is?

BOB: I say that I'm gonna sue the cocksucker. You say no. I mean. What in the hell *possesses* a man. To *treat* you like that: Do you see? It's *cruel*. Jol. *They're cruel*. They were *cruel* toward us, and if there's such a thing as "abuse," we got it. And *your* problem is . . .

JOLLY: I know what my problem is . . .

BOB: . . . your problem . . .

JOLLY: I know what my problem is . . .

BOB: *Your* problem is: You could not face the fact. They didn't love you. And that's your problem. That they did not love us. *(Pause)*

JOLLY: They loved *you*, Buub.

Middle of the night. BOB *and* JOLLY.

JOLLY: "If you don't want it . . ."

BOB: "No, no, no, I *like* it."

JOLLY: "Waal, if you *don't* like it, you can take it back."

BOB: "I like it."

JOLLY: "Waal. If you *don't*. If you find . . ."

BOB: "No, I *Like* it. I *do*. I think that it's . . ."

JOLLY: "Waal, your mother and I, only want to *say* . . ."

BOB: "I think that it's . . ."

JOLLY: "You take it back. We 'saved the slip'. . . and . . ."

BOB: . . . fucking *right* I'm going to take it back. Because what would I *do* with it?

JOLLY: You remember the skis?

62

BOB: The skis.

JOLLY: I remember the skis. I wanted the skis. *(Pause)* I wanted skis that year.

BOB: You don't ski, Jol.

JOLLY: *Why* don't I ski? Bobby? *(Pause)* Oh shit. *(Sighs)* I just, you know, the thing of it, the thing of it is, I just wanted some skis. Would it have killed them to've given me a pair of skis? Was that so ludicrous? A monster like myself? Was that so . . . *(Pause)*

BOB: *(Softly)* . . . yes . . .

JOLLY: Christmas Day. *(Pause)* Christmas Day.

BOB: I know.

JOLLY: She . . .

BOB: Wait, wait, I remember.

JOLLY: You . . . ?

BOB: I remember . . .

JOLLY: You remember what?

BOB: Christmas Day. A plaid . . . a . . . a plaid something.

JOLLY: A . . .

BOB: . . . that they gave me.

JOLLY: . . . yes?

BOB: A plaid . . .

JOLLY: A reversible raincoat.

BOB: That's right.

JOLLY: A reversible raincoat.

BOB: . . . what did I do?

JOLLY: Monday morning. Took it back to Fields.

BOB: I took it back to Fields.

JOLLY: And traded it in.

BOB: That's right.

JOLLY: For what?

BOB: I . . . ? What? No, I've forgotten. Oh, my God. Jol. For what, then, a year . . . ?

JOLLY: . . . easily . . . easily . . .

BOB: For a *year.* "Where is that raincoat, Bubby . . . ?"

JOLLY: ". . . we gave you for Christmas. That you liked so much?"

BOB: "I left it at the . . ." Ah. Ah. Wait. Wait. Jol. Wait, wait, wait. I went back to Fields.

JOLLY: Um hmm.

BOB: TO SEE COULD I BUY BACK THAT COAT.

JOLLY: That's right.

BOB: . . . could I buy back the raincoat.

JOLLY: That's right, Buuby.

BOB: Could I buy back the Fucking Raincoat to stop the questions as to where was the raincoat. That I was so grateful for.

JOLLY: . . . that's right.

BOB: That stupid raincoat. And that woman at Fields. Sent to fucking *Germany* to see, could they replace that raincoat.

JOLLY: That's right, Bobby.

BOB: And calling her back. And calling her back Thursday, and oh, what a pathetic fucking thing. *(Pause)* My plaid. My Plaid Reversible Raincoat. *(Pause)*

JOLLY: And, you know, I'm thinking, all of this, "If you don't *like* it, you can take it back . . ." If they had *loved* us. Mightn't they have *known* what we might want? I know what *my* kids want. *(Pause)* I know what *my* kids want. It's not that difficult. It's Just Not. I'm sorry. Carl says . . . Carl, say what you will. I'm sorry, every weekend, Every weekend. You know what we *did* last weekend? They had friends sleep over. We made *popcorn*. We made *fudge*. Next morning we made *pancakes*. You know, you know, I turned into a fine cook.

BOB: I know you did.

JOLLY: No, I mean, you ain't seen *nothing* here . . .

BOB: It was fantastic . . .

JOLLY: I mean a *fine* cook.

BOB: Jol, I had the dinner . . .

JOLLY: That was nothing.

BOB: No. It was fantastic.

JOLLY: No, I mean, Carl, you know, I wanted to do it, for him . . .

BOB: . . . uh huh . . .

JOLLY: Because before *Carl* you know . . .

BOB: Uh huh . . .

JOLLY: Before *Carl* . . . I . . .

BOB: I remember, Quiche Soup . . .

JOLLY: . . . I couldn't Drop an Egg.

BOB: Uh huh . . .

JOLLY: Why *should* I . . . ? Hummm? *She* never taught me . . . She never taught me a *thing* . . . I'm in here, the girls. *Every night* . . . Every Night I'm in here . . .

BOB: I saw them.

JOLLY: And they're learning to cook.

BOB: I know.

JOLLY: You see, Bob? Do you see? This is a *family*. *(Pause)* *And some day*, Bob. I'm going to be dead. Some day, *they* are going, they are going to be in a kitchen. And they're going to say. To their girls . . . "*My* mom . . ." *(Pause)* Because this is a Family. You see? "My mom used to do it this way." *(Pause)* "This is what my mom taught me." *(Pause)* And every week-end. We had a four-hour session of, we played *Monopoly*. We, God forgive us, we went *bowling*, we . . .

BOB: . . . the kids seem so . . .

JOLLY: . . . we rented a *film* we thought they and their friends would enjoy. And Carl, God bless that man, do you hear?

BOB: Yes.

JOLLY: God *bless* him. And they'd say: "Jol: *Jolly*. We, waaal, he just . . ." And "We don't feel . . ."

BOB: Uh huh . . .

JOLLY: "Your mother and I. 'Just Don't Feel' that *Carl* is the Right Sort."

BOB: Mmm.

JOLLY: The Right Sort. The right fucking sort. Huh? For
who? For a piece of shit like me. For a piece of shit
they *despised*. Like me.

BOB: . . . mmm . . .

JOLLY: Am I wrong? For us. And what in the world gave
them that right? Who never thought a *moment* of my
happiness . . . ? Eh? And the *finest* and the *best man*,
and he *loved* me, you understand? That was the thing,
do you see, that disqualified him, Bob. He loved me.
That was what they hated, Bob. For how could a man
who loved *me* be any good? BUT WHOSE MAR-
RIAGE WORKED— *(Pause)* WHOSE MAR-
RIAGE WORKED? Out of the *pack* of them. Three
generations. And I don't mean you, Buub . . .

BOB: No, I . . .

JOLLY: No, I don't mean you. I mean of them. Who Had
the Marriage That Worked? And it's been, what has it
been, "easy"?

BOB: No.

JOLLY: You are Fucking in Hell *Right* it hasn't. And, you
know. When we thought we would have to move. Out
of *work*. And she'd come, "Mom" . . . She'd come to
see us . . . "Mom" . . . *(Pause)*

BOB: It's okay, Jol. *(Pause)* It's okay. *(Pause)* It's okay, Jol.

JOLLY: Gimme a cigarette. *(Pause. He gives her one.)* I can't smoke these.

BOB: Break the filter.

JOLLY: I can't smoke these.

BOB: Yes, you can. *(She smokes.)*

JOLLY: When we were moving. We Had No Cash, Buub.

BOB: I know. *(Pause)*

JOLLY: And she would come *(Pause)* And I'd say, "Mom . . . you know . . ." she'd first, she'd say, "What do the kids need?" And I'd say "Shoes. They need shoes." *(Pause)* Well, *you* know how kids . . .

BOB: I know . . .

JOLLY: . . . grow out of shoes.

BOB: I know.

JOLLY: *You* know what they cost . . .

BOB: Yes.

JOLLY: Uh huh. "The Kids Need Shoes." The end of her stay, she would give them, God bless her, these, two, *incredibly* expensive, what are they, "vanity" sets. A desk. A desk to put on makeup . . . a "vanity set"?

BOB: . . . I don't know . . .

JOLLY: And I would say . . . *Carl* would say "forget about it." I . . . I'd say . . . No. "Mom . . . Mom . . ." *(Pause)* "Mom . . ." And the fucking *skis*. The *Christmas* skis. One thousand generations we've been Jews. My mother marries a sheigetz and we're celebrating Christmas.

BOB: . . . hey.

JOLLY: . . . huh?

BOB: Mockeys with a Mistletoe . . .

JOLLY: Isn't it . . .

BOB: Yes. It is. *(Pause)*

JOLLY: Jingle Bells. *(Pause)* Ah, what the hell. *(Pause)* And The Big Present. *(Pause)*

BOB: I remember.

JOLLY: I'm sure that you do.

BOB: The Big Present.

JOLLY: "Waal, we've opened *everything* . . ."

BOB: "Oh, *wait* a second . . . 'What Is That Behind the Door.'"

JOLLY: And the fucking skis year it was this expensive, this, Red Leather Briefcase. And I was behaving badly. I was behaving oh so badly. And the one time in my life I said "no." And I said "no." God *knows* where I got the courage. I said *no*. And I was "behaving hysterically." I got sent to my room. And "why must I ruin these occasions?"

BOB: Why did you ruin those occasions, Jol?

JOLLY: Well, that's right. I *ruined* them . . . I *ruined* them . . . because I was an Ungrateful Child. Why did *you* ruin them, Buub?

BOB: Because I was an ungrateful child.

JOLLY: I know that you were. *(Pause)* You know, and I *carried*, I had to *carry* that fucking red briefcase for three or four years, all day, every day, full of books, These Are Your Skis. Did I tell you . . .

BOB: What?

JOLLY: I had a dream about her.

BOB: About Mom . . .

JOLLY: Uh huh. *(Pause)* I'll tell you later. Can I tell you later. You know, because, what was I saying? *(Pause)* Hm . . .

BOB: The Red Briefcase.

JOLLY: Yes. *(Pause)* You know, the girls. So adore having you here.

BOB: It's good to be here.

JOLLY: You . . . it's good of you to come.

BOB: Jol . . .

JOLLY: No, I know that . . .

BOB: Jol, I've been, well *fuck* "remiss." . . . It's been criminal of me not to . . .

JOLLY: I know. You've got a Busy Life . . .

BOB: No, I've just . . .

JOLLY: Buub . . .

BOB: Hey, I've been *lazy*. I'm sorry. I *owe it* to you. I've been . . .

JOLLY: . . . and I know it's been a difficult time for you, Buub . . . *(Pause)*

BOB: And so I came here to get Comfort.

JOLLY: Times of stress, you . . .

BOB: Isn't that "selfish" of me . . . ?

JOLLY: . . . times of stress, you . . . We need comfort. You think that you can do without it? You can't. *(Pause)* You can't, Bob. *(Pause)* No one . . . *(Pause)* Carl and I . . . you know, many times . . . *(Pause)*

BOB: How are you getting on?

JOLLY: We're *(Pause)* Hey, what the fuck are you going to expect. From the Sort of a Background That We Come From. It's a miracle that we can Wind our Watch. *(Pause)* That's what Carl said about you. And, you know . . . how *good* you're doing.

BOB: He said . . .

74

JOLLY: He said that he knows. How incredibly *difficult* this has been for you, and he thinks that you are doing, that he thinks that you are doing well. And *that's* the man, you understand . . . that's the man they made *fun* of. That they said "wasn't good enough for me." *(Pause) Fuck* them. Fuck the *lot* of them. *(Pause)* And carried that fucking *bookbag* around for three years. *(Pause)* What are you gonna do?

BOB: About?

JOLLY: About your life. *(Pause)*

BOB: I don't know.

JOLLY: You don't know. Tell me. You gonna go back to her?

BOB: I don't know.

JOLLY: 'Cause I wanted to tell you. If you *do*. No one's going to think you foolish. I swear to you.

BOB: I'm not going back to her.

JOLLY: If you *do*. *(Pause)* I'm not saying you *should* . . .

BOB: I un . . .

JOLLY: Or you should *not*. But if you *do*, always . . .

BOB: . . . I know . . .

JOLLY: You remember, Bob. Carl, Carl said it: He said it, baby. You, you can *Kill the Pope*, and you are wel . . .

BOB: I'm not going to go back . . .

JOLLY: . . . if you *should*. And I am not "plumping" for it.

BOB: I know. *(Pause)*

JOLLY: I WANT ONE THING. And that is: The thing that is best for you. Period. Paragraph. And the rest of the world can go to hell. I don't give a fuck. I'm too old. *(Pause)* And there you have it and that's the story of it. *(Pause)* All I want to say . . . *(Long pause)* . . . Fella comes up to me, I'm driving, fella comes up to me I'm drivin' the girls somewhere, "Don't you know," No. "Did you know. This is a One-way Street . . ." I'm . . . never in my life, Bob. I'm sick. I'm a sick woman. I know that. I'm aware of that, how could I not be. My mind is racing "Did you know," "Didn't you know . . ." Did I drive down on PUR-POSE? I did *not* know . . . IS YOUR QUES-TION . . . what? The proper, I would say, response, is "One-way Street!" Smiles. One way. You, we would *assume*, did not know that you are, why *would* I, and even, I HAD, how *terrible* is that. Some piece of shit JUST LIKE ME. Whether or *not* I knew, your . . .

your "rights" end with "this is a one-way street," and what I MAY HAVE KNOWN is none of your *concern*, and FUCK YOU, and I'm SEETHING at this, this emasculated piece of shit who has to take out his *aggression* on some haggard, sexless, unattractive *house-wife*, with her *kids* in her station wagon . . . *(Pause)* and this is my fantasy life. *(Pause)* A rich, "full" life. *(Pause)*

BOB: You should go to bed.

JOLLY: Why should I go to bed?

BOB: Because you have a husband up there. *(Pause)*

JOLLY: I thought you gave up smoking.

BOB: You know, some times I can't . . . I can't, it seems I can't . . . *(Pause)* Oh, God, I get so *sad* sometimes, Jol. I can't, it seems, getting up from the *table* . . . *(Pause)* I wake up in the night. "Where am I?" Three times in a night. And I saw that I was waking up.

JOLLY: To go pee the kids.

BOB: To pee the kids. You get a Red apple.

JOLLY: Your kids are going to be okay.

BOB: No, they won't. Of *course* they won't. *We're* not okay . . .

Morning. CARL. BOB *comes in.*

CARL: How did you sleep?

BOB: Like a rock or like a baby. *(Pause)*

CARL: *(To Bob)* You know, he *dumped* this stuff here.

BOB: Jolly was telling me. *(Pause)* What was it?

CARL: It was *trash*, you'd say. It was . . .

BOB: . . . *my* stuff . . .

CARL: Your stuff. Stuff you couldn't want. Canceled
checks. Twenty years old. It was nothing anyone could
ever want to keep. Just some . . . "trash," really . . .
(Pause) You know. There was so much stuff Jolly
wanted. Some of your mother's . . . When he sold the
house. *(Pause)*

BOB: How can you put up with it?

CARL: Well what "it," then . . . ?

BOB: The misfortune of our family. Do I overstate the case . . . ?

CARL: Oh, I don't . . . that's a very personal question, isn't it?

BOB: Yes. It is.

CARL: *(Pause)* Well, you know. I love Jolly.

BOB: . . . are we that . . . are we that . . .

CARL: That what?

BOB: Are we . . . you know, I feel so *pathetic* sometimes, Carl.

CARL: Well . . .

BOB: No, what can you say about it? *(JOLLY enters.)*

JOLLY: Sleep well?

BOB: Yes.

JOLLY: How well?

BOB: Very well.

JOLLY: Why?

BOB: 'Cause I feel "safe" here.

JOLLY: How safe?

BOB: Very safe.

JOLLY: Safer than Other Places . . . ?

BOB: Yes.

JOLLY: Safer than Anyplace Else in the World?

BOB: Yes.

JOLLY: Well, hell then.

BOB: Hey.

JOLLY: That's what I'm telling you. *(Pause)*. The girls say good-bye.

BOB: Good-bye to *them*. *(Pause)*

JOLLY: Um. Call me when you get where you're going.

BOB: Why?

JOLLY: So I'll know you got there. *(Pause)* You okay?

BOB: Yeah.

JOLLY: Thanks for coming.

BOB: Oh, hell.

JOLLY: No, no. Thank you. We . . .

CARL: Jol, he wanted to come.

JOLLY: Was I talking to you . . . ?

CARL: No. Good-bye, Bob.

BOB: Good-bye, Carl.

JOLLY: Did you know, this stupid shmuck. Drove two hours to Hillcrest to pick up three boxes of, turned out to be, drafts of your *term* papers, something, junior high. *(Pause)* Carl . . . ?

CARL: Bye, Hon.

JOLLY: . . . canceled *checks.* Something. Cocksucker: He calls up: "We have some stuff of Bob's . . ." Carl drives there to pick it up. Like fools. We, he goes over there. It's garbage. That they saved. We're s'posed to take it. *(Sighs)*

CARL: Bye, Hon.

JOLLY: See you at six.

CARL: Yes.

JOLLY: The girls at gymnastics.

CARL: Yes, I know. Bye, Buub.

BOB: I'll see you, Carl.

CARL: You hang on.

BOB: All right.

CARL: Thank you for coming.

BOB: It was good to come.

JOLLY: He was glad to come. He was glad to come. One time in nnnnnnn years, you *should* be glad to come. A house full of folks who love you.

CARL: Good-bye, Bob. *(To* JOLLY*)* Bye, Sweetheart. *(He exits.)*

JOLLY: Don't go. *(Pause)* We could go back. To Seventy-first Street is where we could go. To the Jeffrey Theatre. And Saturday kiddie shows. Twenty-five cartoons and a western. For a quarter. And the Chocolate Phosphate at J. Leslie Rosenblum's,

"Every Inch a Drugstore." Do you remember? Dad, he used to take us there?

BOB: Yes. I do.

JOLLY: Do you remember how it smelled?

BOB: Yes.

JOLLY: And we'd go to the Peter Pan Restaurant. On the corner of Jeffrey, and get a Francheezie, and the french fries, and a cherry Coke. And we would go to the South Shore Country Club, where they wouldn't let us in. And we would sit in the window in the den, and Dad would come home every night, and we would light the candles on Friday, and we would do all those things, and all those things would be true and that's how we would grow up. And the old men, who said that they remembered Nana. Back in Poland. And, oh. Fuck it. Oh the hell with it.

BOB: I never came to see you.

JOLLY: *I don't care* . . .

BOB: . . . I never came . . .

JOLLY: No. I don't care . . . *(Pause)* Oh, Bobby. *(Pause)* Oh, God . . .

CARL: Well . . . *(Exits)*

JOLLY: And I'm having this dream. How's *this* for dreams . . . ? They're knocking on my door. All of them. "Let me in," and I know that they want to kill me. *Mother: Mother's* voice, from just beyond the door: "Julia, Let Me In." "I will not let them hurt you . . ." the sweetest voice. "You are my *child* . . ." and it goes on. "I won't let them hurt you, darling . . . you are my *child.* You are my *child.* Open the door. Oh. *Julia.* I will not let them Hurt You. OH. My Dear . . ." I open the door, this sweetest voice, and there is *Mom,* with this *expression* on her face . . . *(Pause)* And she wants to kill me. *(Pause)*

BOB: Well.

JOLLY: . . . and I knew that she did. So why did I open the door . . . ? *(Pause)* Isn't that the thing of it.

BOB: "Thank God it was only a dream . . ."

JOLLY: Yes. *(Pause)* Isn't that a mercy . . . ? *(Carl reenters. Pause. Picks up sheet of paper.)* The address of the gymnastics.

CARL: Mm.

JOLLY: What a good man.

CARL: What are you doing?

JOLLY: We're being bad. We've been bad. We're being punished. And we're going to go to our rooms. And cannot come out until we're prepared to make, a . . . what is it . . . ?

BOB: A Complete and Contrite . . .

JOLLY: A Complete and Contrite Apology. *(Pause)*

CARL: Do you want me to stay home?

JOLLY: No. Thank you. Bobby will be here a while, you see. And he's the only one who knows. *(Pause)* 'Cause he was *there* . . .

DEENY

DEENY: *(Pause)* They say there's going to be a frost tonight.

BOB: Do they?

DEENY: Yes.

BOB: Y'always liked that.

DEENY: Yes. I did. It made me wish I had a garden. *(Pause)*

BOB: Uh hmm.

DEENY: You know?

BOB: Yes.

DEENY: And you could go out to it, the morning; and see, well, you could go out to it the night before, and "cover" things . . . cover things, or "bring them in." *(Pause)* You could, certain spots, they put smudge—is that the word? Smudge pots, you know, not a very pretty word, is it?

BOB: No.

DEENY: To keep the plants warm. *(Pause)* But I was saying, in the morning. You would go out, do you know, even, well, I was going to say To Get Up Early, but I think that if you were a gardener you probably *would* be up early. Do you think?

BOB: Yes.

DEENY: . . . out of *love*. *(Pause)* Rather than what? Rather than . . . what?

BOB: Rather than a sense of duty.

DEENY: Yes.

BOB: . . . or the two would be one.

DEENY: Well, that is the thing I'm *saying. Isn't* it?

BOB: I know.

DEENY: That would be love.

BOB: Indeed it would.

DEENY: And I had a vision of *coffee*. Coffee, certainly . . . I *thought*, you see, I *thought* that the unfortunate thing about it was that it closed us off. And that *coffee* . . .

BOB: . . . yes.

DEENY: *Coffee*, or *cigarettes* tended to . . .

BOB: . . . to . . .

DEENY: . . . *paralyze.*

BOB: Yes.

DEENY: . . . natural functions, you see, in that the one, with the digestion, or the other, with the lungs, cut down our . . .

BOB: . . . our . . .

DEENY: . . . abilities . . . to . . . to . . . *(Pause)* you know, to *use* the world, I think—those things of the world we could take in: food, or air, you know, and *use* them. Perhaps. So we say, "It's too much." I had a vision of a frosty morning. Myself with a cigarette. And with a cup of coffee. Smoking. As I look out of my window. And I see a garden. In this garden there are plants that I have planted and perhaps I have raised them from seeds or cuttings, do you know? The way they do . . . ?

BOB: Tell me.

DEENY: To raise them inside, you know, from the year before. They call it "forcing." Or they call something else forcing, and they call this something else. *(Pause)* But that's a nice word, isn't it?

BOB: What?

DEENY: Forcing.

BOB: Forcing. Yes.

DEENY: If you talk about it. As, you know, as "bringing out." These little green cups. Seeds that you have put in by the radiator. In the most... *(Pause)* Wait a moment. *(Pause)* In the most safe and in the most protected of all settings in the world. *Otherwise,* they would not be born, *(Pause)* you see; and that is what I saw when I looked out the window. *(Pause)* I think about sex sometimes, and I think about all the times you think of a thing and vary between thinking that "it is a mystery," and "it is a convenience." And many times, you do not know which of the two it is. Do you think of that?

BOB: I think that of various things.

DEENY: Of what?

BOB: Of life, of work. Of sex, of success.

DEENY: Of *all* things.

BOB: I think.

DEENY: You go back and forth.

BOB: Yes.

DEENY: Without a certainty.

BOB: Or with one which changes.

DEENY: . . . and I think about the stupid *molecules*. Whatever the smallest unit is. They always tell us, in the newspapers, every day, some new unit, and you think, "surely *this* is, the thing you tell us now, must be the smallest unit." Or, "you should," you think, "you should confess that there *is* no end to it. That there *is* no smallest unit, and it is your *science* that is lacking," do you know? ". . . either the *instruments* or the humility to say, 'There is no end to it.'" And oriental faiths, you know, posit a *pathway*, or say there is an extra *nerve* in the spine, science cannot find, the "third eye," they're talking about. Or, or an "aura," and I think: "Yes, well, of course, you can approach it through *spiritual* practice," you know, what, what, I suppose that you would call it "faith"; it isn't that much different from believing something we see in the newspaper.

BOB: Faith.

DEENY: Not much, really. Or believing some, some spiri-
tual thing. It's just something that someone says is
true. And you say, "Yes. I'll believe that that's true."
(Pause) But having lost the feeling that things will
right themselves. *(Pause)* What? It becomes harder.
Because I never, more importantly, nor, will I. I never
planted a garden, nor *will* I plant a garden, and when I
question myself as to *why*, I have no answer.
"Would it give you pleasure?"
"Yes."
"Would you enjoy it?"
"Yes."
"Would it be difficult to do?"
"No."
"Then why do you not *do* it?"
And there is no answer, but, do you know, do you
know what I mean, but it is . . . waiting . . . that's a
funny word . . . it's waiting, waiting, just beyond . . .
you know, it's in the back of my mind. "It's
because . . ." What? What is it because? It's too much
trouble? No. No, you see, I say to myself, that it's the
opposite of trouble. It's *joy*. Well, then, I say. Well, then,
draw yourself up and *do* it. And I say "perhaps I will."
Perhaps I will.

BOB: . . . that things will not come right . . .

DEENY: Well, they *won't, will* they . . . ? *(Pause)* In the
world. The, the, the, world . . . and I was talking
about "faith." And you say "this is ending." Well,

then, there's *another* thing. And that will take its place. And sometimes that's okay. But then, sometimes, that's just cold comfort. *Isn't* it?

BOB: Yes.

DEENY: How d'you think I'm doing at my job?

BOB: I think you're doing fine.

DEENY: Yes. I do, too. I enjoy it so much.

BOB: I can see that you do.

DEENY: And, do you know, as you grow older—all the things you said, "They must be true, because they're 'platitudes.'" Or, what is it, what is it they say? That's not what they say. What do they say?

BOB: It's a cliché because it's true.

DEENY: "It got to be a cliché, because it was true." But if you think about it, if that's its reward, that's a poor reward. Isn't it? It was *true* . . . what it used to be was *true*, and did it so well that it *got* to be the *other* thing, which is that we ignore it, but what was I saying?

BOB: That it is true, *although* we have heard it so often that we tend to discount it. That to do something truly well you have to love it.

DEENY: . . . and they think so at work, too, because they're going to offer me, oh, you don't want to hear it, you may want to hear it, I don't want to tell it; how could it, do you know, how could it *interest* you? Because it's like you're walking through a part of town, and you say, "You see that house? I used to live there." "Really." What can it *mean* to them? Nothing. It means something to *you*, you see, as it should. *(Pause)* But the other person, they feel lonely. Or I wanted to say, "It's not much, but it's *mine*." *(Pause)*

BOB: I know.

DEENY: I know you know. *(Pause)* "It's not much" . . . eh? "But it's . . ." And what *could* it mean to you? You know? As the phrase is "anyway," because it truly couldn't. It's nothing. It's . . . a bit of *buying. Ordering*, mainly, accountancy . . . "Accountancy"? "Accounting" . . . Bookkeeping . . . I keep track of some things. There really is a bit of buying. Everyone thinks that they've got good taste. Everyone thinks "Everyone thinks that they've got good taste, but I *have* got good taste . . ." *(Pause)* But I *have* got good taste. And I like it, and they like me, and there you have it. What a success story. How's *your* life?

BOB: As you see.

DEENY: I was thinking of tribes that *mutilate* themselves, and it occurred to me, that, perhaps, when they *do* it, they... *(Pause)* they get *pleasure* from it. Those tribes that... tattoo their faces, or they stretch their lips, you know, or *necks*, or the terrible things they do to their sexual, their sexual equipment; but I thought, if you know that this is terrible, as you do, and know you are frightened, which is to say, you *are* frightened, and you know that *it is the community* that forces you, then might you not feel, might you not feel, as they *did* it, you see ...: "Yes. Yes. I surrender." And you *die.* You undergo the pain of, the pain of, the pain of giving birth to yourself. And that *sorrow* of *years* ...

BOB: ... yes I understand.

DEENY: ... that sorrow of years. Is condensed, do you see, into a *ceremony.* And then it is over. *(Long pause)* Looking at the "old thing." Looking at *regret.* What is it we hope to gain by looking at it? Do we think it *raises* us ...? No. Do you know, it's not important.

BOB: What is important? *(Pause)*

DEENY: What is important? *(Pause)* You know, couldn't you say of *anything* that it is folly? Except passion. While you're feeling it, and afterward, *especially* of that. That it is folly. *(Pause)* That everything is folly.

BOB: Yes. You could say that.

DEENY: People with sorrow in their eyes ...

BOB: . . . yes . . .

DEENY: . . . you know . . . people you wouldn't be *drawn* to when you were young.

BOB: No.

DEENY: You wouldn't see them.

BOB: No.

DEENY: But they would see *you*. Maybe they'd be *attracted* to you. *(Pause)* Some older person. Looking down.

BOB: Yes, looking down.

DEENY: But could not *have* them.

BOB: Who could not?

DEENY: The older person.

BOB: Have what?

DEENY: Have that younger love.

BOB: Have *passion* . . .

DEENY: No.

BOB: Because . . . ?

DEENY: Well, *you* know why then, *don't* you. Because it had passed. Well. And the *things* we did. And things we said. To other lovers. And the *jokes,* the private jokes, you know, and *poignancies;* and all the revenge we foreswore, *and that we could not have.* Always, and *turning,* don't we? Toward death—Do you think? Do you think so? *(Pause)* And, you know, and the things we'd given up. When you elect it's consolation to grow up. And it *is* consolation. *But So What?* And the things we kept *till we grew sick of them.* The treasured pivots of our *world*—until . . . *(Pause)*

BOB: "Until one day . . ."

DEENY: *Oh* yes. *(Pause)* I never knew what you wanted. *(Pause)* I thought I knew. *(Pause)* I thought that I knew. *(Pause) Finally . . . (Pause)* And I said. *(Pause)* They say there's going to be a frost.

BOB: Well, then, I am sure that there is.

DEENY: I am sure that there is, too. *(Pause) Despite* the fact that they say it.

BOB: That's my girl.

DEENY: And it will grow cold. You know, and you used to say, "How Jolly." I'm sure you still say it; though to other people, of course, and I don't blame you. For why should we change? Do you know? If there were something I could do for you, I'd do it. *(Pause)* Or for myself. Even to proclaim, you know, that this world is a shit hole. If I just could find it true. *(Pause)* Did you come to say good-bye? *(Pause)*

BOB: Yes.

DEENY: Good-bye, then.

BOB: Good-bye. *(Pause)*

DEENY: Good-bye, then, love. *(Pause)*

BOB: Good-bye, love.

Printed in the United States
by Baker & Taylor Publisher Services